Bailey's Halloween Tea Party by Roni Zulu
Published by Zulu Studios
www.ronizulu.com

Story and Illustration by Roni Zulu.

Hardback ISBN: 978-1-7369831-0-2
Library of Congress Control Number: 2021941170

Bailey's Halloween Tea Party

This is Bailey and her cat Bean.
Bailey loves Halloween because it is a time she can be
whatever she wants to be.

She can be a racecar driver, a princess,
a pirate, or a witch.
She can be whatever she wants to be.

It's the day before Halloween and Bailey
is having breakfast with her parents.

"Mom, Dad, what should I be for Halloween?"
asked Bailey.
Her parents said, "Bailey,
you can be whatever you want to be."

"I don't know what I want to be," said Bailey.
"I'll ask some of my friends what they think I should be.
This will be fun; I have so many different friends
I'll get lots of wonderful ideas for what I can be."

Bailey went to see her friend, Mr. Kim,
who runs the town general store.

"Mr. Kim, tomorrow is Halloween; what should I be?"
asked Bailey.
Mr. Kim replied, "Bailey, you can be whatever
you want to be! Here is a lollipop for you."
Bailey said, "Thank you," and then asked,
"Can I please have another lollipop for Mrs. Brockman?
She likes candy and I'm going to see her today."
"Oh no," said Mr. Kim, "She has green eyes,
I don't like green eyes."
Bailey said, "Oh! Thanks anyway."

Bailey went to see her friend, Mrs. Brockman,
who is the town seamstress.

"Mrs. Brockman, tomorrow is Halloween;
what should I be?" asked Bailey.
Mrs. Brockman replied, "Bailey, you can be whatever
you want to be!
Here is a pair of mittens to keep you warm."
Bailey said, "Thank you," and then asked,
"Can I please have another pair of mittens for
Mr. Sam? It's cold at his place and
I'm going to see him today."
"Oh no," said Mrs. Brockman, "He has black hair,
I don't like black hair."
Bailey said, "Oh! Thanks anyway."

Bailey went to see her friend, Mr. Sam,
who is the town artist.

"Mr. Sam, tomorrow is Halloween; what should I be?"
asked Bailey.
Mr. Sam replied, "Bailey, you can be
whatever you want to be!
Here are some crayons for you."
Bailey said, "Thank you," and then asked,
"Can I please have some crayons for Mr. Carlo?
He likes pretty colors and I'm going
to see him today."
"Oh no," said Mr. Sam, "He has a mustache,
I don't like mustaches."
Bailey said, "Oh! Thanks anyway."

Bailey went to see her friend, Mr. Carlo,
who is the town barber.

"Mr. Carlo, tomorrow is Halloween; what should I be?"
asked Bailey.
Mr. Carlo replied, "Bailey, you can be
whatever you want to be!
Here is a comb for you."
Bailey said, "Thank you," and then asked,
"Can I please have another comb for
Miss Rachel? She has beautiful hair and
I'm going to see her today."
"Oh no,'" said Mr. Carlo, "She has freckles,
I don't like freckles."
Bailey said, "Oh! Thanks anyway."

Bailey went to see her friend, Miss Rachel,
who is the town librarian.

"Miss Rachel, tomorrow is Halloween; what should I be?"
asked Bailey.
Miss Rachel replied, "Bailey, you can be
whatever you want to be!
Here is a book for you."
Bailey said, "Thank you," and then asked,
"Can I please have another book for
Mr. Kim? He likes to read and I'm going back
to his general store to buy Halloween candy."
"Oh no," said Miss Rachel, "He has big ears,
I don't like big ears."
Bailey said, "Oh! Thanks anyway."

Bailey was walking home after buying candy
for Halloween. She passed by a house where people
were having a party in the front yard.
They were all dressed in costumes and masks.

They all said to Bailey, "Hello there, please come and
join our Halloween tea party."

Bailey sat at the table and gave everyone some candy and then asked, "Tomorrow is Halloween, everyone; what should I be?"

"You can be whatever you want to be", said one of the people at the table. Another person at the table said, "Halloween isn't until tomorrow but we all have so much fun with each other wearing our costumes, we decided to start today!"

Bailey replied, "Your costumes are very nice but I can't see your faces because you're wearing masks; what are your names?"

No one knew who the others at the table were
because their faces were covered.
Then everyone took off their masks.

"My name is Mr. Kim", said Mr. Kim.

Then Mrs. Brockman said,
"My name is Mrs. Brockman".

Mr. Sam told everyone,
"My name is Mr. Sam".

"My name is Mr. Carlo", said Mr. Carlo.

And finally, Miss Rachel said,
"My name is Miss Rachel",

Bailey told all of them,

"When I came to see all of you,
Mr. Kim didn't like Mrs. Brockman
because she has green eyes.

Mrs. Brockman didn't like Mr. Sam
because he has black hair.

Mr. Sam didn't like Mr. Carlo
because he has a mustache.

Mr. Carlo didn't like Miss Rachel
because she has freckles.

And Miss Rachel didn't like Mr. Kim
because he has big ears."

Then Mr. Kim gave Mrs. Brockman a lollipop
and said, "You have pretty green eyes!"

Mrs. Brockman gave Mr. Sam some mittens
and said, "You have nice black hair!"

Mr. Sam gave Mr. Carlo some crayons
and said, "What a wonderful mustache you have."

Mr. Carlo gave Miss Rachel a comb
and said, "Those freckles look great with
your beautiful hair!"

And Miss Rachel gave Mr. Kim a book
and said, "I really like your ears!"

Bailey said as she was leaving,
"I'm glad all of you took off your masks
so we could see who you really are.
I have to go home now, thank you for the tea.
Goodbye!"

Bailey walked back home and her parents
were very happy to see her.

"Bailey, tomorrow is Halloween...what are you
going to be?", asked her parents.

Bailey answered,
"I can be whatever I want to be!"

Happy
Halloween!

CPSIA information can be obtained
at www.ICGtesting.com
Printed in the USA
BVHW020946030721
610976BV00023B/983